First Edition

Copy rights 2023. Noble and Rational

Noble and Rational

PO Box 18688

Austin, TX, 78760

God the creator, or by chance?

I know the topic of the book is very provocative for atheists, you are going to say, no one can refute atheism in 30 minutes. In fact, I can refute atheism in 4 seconds only, get ready for it: -

The universe can't exist without the laws of physics, and the laws of physics can't exist without intelligence. I just did, in 4 seconds. But that is only for those who understand the value of the laws of physics, if you don't, it's your problem not mine.

I know if you are atheist, you are now so angry, and so mad at me.

Chill out dude, let me cool you off with this Very easy, very quick challenge, if you can overcome the challenge, I will make everyone an atheist in 24 hours. I promise and guarantee that for you.

You atheists, you keep saying over millions of years, over millions of years, and over millions of years. Thanks to computers, we will simulate for you the concept of millions of years, in hours, in fact, in minutes. It only takes computers minutes to simulate your millions of years concept, because they run really, fast.

The challenge

Write an authentic, cheat proof, and testable, computer software that will RANDOMLY throw some dice 60000 times, and in the first 10000 times, must give us only the number 1, then in the second 10000 times, must give us only the number 2. And in the in the third 10000 times, must give us only the number 3, and in the fourth 10000 times, must give us only the number 4, and in the fifth 10000 times, must give us only the number 5, and the rest 10000 times, to give us only the number 6. Don't test the results until all 60000 are done. Keep repeating until you get all the right 60000. Once you do get that, I will make everyone an atheist. Don't worry, you do your thing, and I will do my thing.

This is a fair test for both sides. Keep the computer running for as long as you want, many days, many months, many years, up to 10 years. Then come share the results with us, by the way you may use up to 1000 computers running the same thing, all at the same time, this way we overcome the concept of over millions of years. You know you will miserably fail.

Ok Folks, the human body and all its functions are billions of times more sophisticated than the 60000-challenge number. But I was very nice, I gave them a HUGE discount, free discount. You Know you can't do it. Did you cool off dude?

Please believers say, "thank you computers". Now stop telling me, if we have lots of monkeys typing stuff, they will produce so and so, my 60000-challenge number resembles that and more. If you dare, go for it.

Can science tell us anything about GOD?

When it comes to GOD, science is MUTE. Only intelligence can lead us to GOD.

Science can't say anything about God for 2 reasons:

First reason, science can only explore testable stuff, but God is untestable.

Second reason, science can only explore things that is part of this universe, but God is not part of this universe, also the soul and its power consciousness are not part of this universe, they only exist in it while you are alive, when you die, they go outside this universe.

Science is nothing more than a man-made tool, made only to explore what is inside this universe. Science jurisdiction only exists inside this universe, but not outside it. Therefor science is useless outside this universe.

So, when are debating an atheist tell him right away science can't tell us anything about God, for those 2 reasons, he will try to say the scientific evidence says so and so, tell him the scientific evidence is science, and science can't say anything about God, science is useless outside this universe.

If you come from a scriptural background like me

Please consider these 3 points:

First Point, I do believe in an evolution that was planned and supervised.

Second point, please consider that the scripture doesn't say that God created everything right away in its final form, which means a planned systematic evolution is possible. Consider these three examples:

Example 1: You were created by God, but not right away in your final form, you started as a sperm and an egg, then took some time for you to become a full human. And that by itself is a planned systematic evolution.

Example 2: the trees didn't become trees in their final form right away, they started as a small seed.

Example 3: the chicken started as an egg, not a chicken right away.

Third point: the word day in ancient middle eastern languages don't always mean a 24 hour period, sometimes it means a long period of time, depends on the context, and people use of the word day, so don't let the limitation of the English language, or any other language bound you to a 24 hour period, in fact if you was born on another planet that has 36 hour day, and you came to visit us on planet earth you will right away understand that the word day doesn't always mean a 24 hour period.

If you are a believer, please don't consider a planned evolution is an argument against God's existence, that is only assumption, in fact everything in the universe is a planned system or part of a planned system, except for the things that we know they are random, like flipping a coin, or throwing some dice, etc.

The atheist mentality

If you are atheist, you are a blind believer.

You are a blind believer in by coincidence, by luck, by chance, by probability, by time, by random mutations, and many others.

You are the number one fan of believing in by coincidence, by coincidence, by coincidence … unlimited number of coincidences.

Don't you dare to put a limit on the number of coincidences that you are willing to accept, you must keep it unlimited?

Those are your golden words, or your magic words, they provide you with a scape rout to avoid acknowledging that intelligence is required for the existence of the universe and all the organized systems in it, like the laws of physics, complex life forms, etc.

Those words are you gods, they will save your theology for you, but only in your mind.

Atheists in fact are polytheists. Because in their minds they took the power and the roll of the true God, and gave them to their new gods, their new gods include:

By coincidence, by luck, by chance, by probability, by time, by random mutations, and many others.

This is my explanation for that, if you take the presidential power and roll of the us president, and you give them to Mr. X, practically, not officially, you make Mr. X a president.

In their minds they took the power and roll of God and gave them to by coincidence, by chance, by luck, by mutations, by probability, by time, etc. And made them their unofficial gods, but officially, they will never acknowledge that they have gods, but they do have unofficial gods.

To explain the existence of life they must depend heavily, heavily, and heavily on those gods.

When it comes to explain how complex life came to exist, they can't cross the border or the fence of by chance or by coincident, by luck, etc. they are stock in the box of by chance, and other boxes, they can't think outside the box, the wall of by chance is the farthest point their thinking may reach, they can't cross that wall, and think beyond coincident, when it comes to explaining how life came to exist, they are stuck in the box, all this, is just because they don't want to acknowledge that intelligence is the maker of life.

In explaining how life came about, they MUST stay away from the word intelligence here, the word intelligence is their biggest enemy, their biggest taboo, their biggest forbidden, their biggest illegal, their biggest fear, their biggest hated to mention word, their biggest nightmare, this word (intelligence) must be avoided at all costs. The same thing with the laws of physics, to explain how they came to be, don't you dare to mention the word intelligence.

When it comes to explaining how life or the laws of physics came to be, you must stay away from the word intelligence. Because this word will instantly destroy their theology. But they love to use the word intelligence for everything else, for everything else the word intelligence is welcomed. But not for those two things, explaining how life came to be or how the laws of physics came to be. Instead, to explain how life came to be, they LOVE to use the words random and luck, these are the most favorite 2 words in their vocabulary, RANDOM and LUCK.

For us believers, we always love to use the word intelligence for everything, in fact we can't have any faith in anything if it is not supported by intelligence.

There are three major types of atheists:

First, those who don't want to believe in God for no reason, period.

Second, those who don't believe in God for certain reasons, like their prayer wasn't answered, or because they got misled, or because of the suffering in the world, etc.

Third, those who don't know why they are atheists.

For laugh

We say in God we trust. Can you guess what they say?

They say in coincidences we trust. But they don't dare to say it in plain words, they say it by implication.

We say in the name of God. You know what they say by implication, (in the name of random and luck).

Everyone knows, to make a complex system you need intelligence, but atheists will say some complex systems, like the universe and its systems and subsystems, or the systems of life don't need intelligence they only need luck. in fact, you need luck to win the lottery, or to understand that those systems need intelligence.

Ok folks let me tell you this story that will apply to most atheists, let us test their blind belief in by coincidence, by coincidence, by coincidence.

THE STORY

I was debating an atheist, I told him I'm only willing to accept three coincidences, I will accept the first one no problem, the second one, I will say ok, like in long word ok that has many o's, the third one I will stop and think for a while before accepting it, but eventually I will. But for the fourth one I will say hey dude (not saying his name, but rather using the word dude). Stop it and go find somebody else. Not me dude.

And then I continued saying:

 If the sun was double the size we wouldn't be here, if it was half the size we wouldn't be here, ok that is a coincidence, not a big deal.

If the distance between planet earth and the sun was doubled, we wouldn't be here, if it was half we wouldn't be here, ok coincident not a big deal.

If planet earth was double the size, too big very bad, if it was half, too small very bad, ok coincident, not a big deal.

If the trees also use oxygen like humans, not CO2, do you think we would be here? How did it happen that trees take our CO2, and give us O2? What if they didn't? Is that a coincidence?

Here comes my second favorite one, if the speed of the rotation of the earth around its axis was double, that means 6 hours for the day and 6 hours for the night, if it was half that means 24 hours for the day and 24 hours for the night, ok just another lucky coincident, not a big deal.

Folks here comes my favorite one, let's stop and think about it.

If you are atheist, don't you dare to tell me this one is a coincidence, don't you even think about it.

My favorite point, my golden point.

If the amount of water on planet earth was doubled, we wouldn't be here, if it was half, most planet earth would be deserted and not fit for human civilization.

I know still they will say the probability is there, but that is only theorical probability in their minds.

Then I moved to give him, in wholesale billions and billions of coincidences.

I told him from the first cell that started (your grandpa), until you became a human, how many RANDOM mutations had happened billions, and billions, and billions of them. I told him I will give you a free discount, I'm not going to worry about all the coincidences that happened to bring up the first cell, that is free discount.

Now for the big question that is going to make it or break it.

How many of those billions, and billions, and billions of random mutations, by coincident, by coincident, again by coincident, and yes by coincident, were the right one for the right reason at the right time. 99.99% of them, BY COINCIDENT, were the right one, for the right reason, at exactly the right time, yes 99.99%.

If you want to argue against this point, go see chapter named (99.99% 50% of 50%)

And he didn't have any problem to blindly, without thinking accept billions of coincidences, and I asked him, how many coincidences you are willing to accept rather than believing in God?

He answered an unlimited number of coincidences.

Now I moved to expose his hypocrisy by asking him this question.

If you come home one day and your girlfriend on the phone and she tells you, by coincident I dialed the wrong number and it is so and so, then the second day you come home she is on the phone, she tells you by coincident I dialed the wrong number and it is so and so, then the third day you come home she is on the phone, she tells you by coincident I dialed the wrong number and it is so and so, and repeated that scenario five times, then I asked him:

How many coincidences are you willing to accept before you suspect something is wrong?

He answered from the first time he will suspect something is wrong.

Then he tried to justify his blind faith in coincidences rather than believing in God even by much worse argument, he said:

May be nature was trying to do so and so:

Right away I told him, this is a great statement, thank you for saying that, but it is great for me not you, then I said, to try anything you need a mind, and if you don't have a mind, you can't try anything.

For the believers

When you debate atheist ask him, if he was in some official science experiment, and every one notices something, and you jump to say, let's not worry about it, this is a coincident, then you guys notice a second thing, and you jump to say, the same thing, then you guys notice a third thing, and you jump to say also the same thing, are they going to keep you in the experiment? Answer, no.

But for the most important question we have, which is who are we? Are we the sons of animals? Or we are standalone humans created by God from dust?

For this question (experiment) everyone in your team will accept your coincidences and keep you in the experiment.

If you are debating atheist, it is better to know if he is willing to accept the existence of God. or he is one of those who don't want to believe in God, period. That will save you time and energy.

You may think the main issue with most atheists is that they don't believe in God, no that is not the main issue with most atheists, the main issue with most atheists, is that they don't want to believe in God, period.

If you are debating, an atheist, tell him to explain how life came to be without using 2 words, random and luck, or their meanings. They can't, for them random and luck are 2 of their gods.

THE FOUR TWINS

The universe consists of four fundamental components (twins). I call them the four brothers or the four twins.

The first fundamental component is the Laws of physics.

The second fundamental component is Time.

The third fundamental component is Space,

The fourth fundamental component is the Stuff, but here I'm talking about matter only. The stuff includes matter, antimatter, dark matter, energy, dark energy, and everything else.

Those four fundamental components came to exist exactly at the same time exactly at the same fraction of a second, at the exact moment of the big bang, (just to let you know, I do believe in the big bang), If anyone of them was missing, life would not exist. If any one of them was late by 1 MS or even a much smaller fraction of a second, then life will not exist.

The laws of physics

The first most important fundamental component of the universe is the laws of physics, the laws of physics have absolute power, authority and control over time space, and matter, and everything else in the universe except life, over life they only have limited control, and if the laws of physics did not exist, then the universe will not exist, because the existence of the universe, you and I depends on the laws of physics to be there in first place.

The laws of physics are the most fundamental component of the universe that gives a chance for everything else to exist. The laws of physics are pre-required for everything else to exist, and without the laws of physics, this universe absolutely can't exist. The laws of physics are the MOTHER OF ALL MOTHERS in the universe except for life. Because life is a new dimension in the universe.

The laws of physics have at least four jobs: -

First, they give the universe, and each particle and sub particle their identities. They tell us what everything is and how it works, the laws of physics work as identity cards for the universe, particles and sub particles and other things.

For example, they tell the electron, you are electron, you must act this way, you must be in that place doing that thing, you must have this charge, you must have this volume, you must have that much weight, and so on. They do it for every particle and sub particle and other stuff. And nothing can disobey the laws of physics.

Second, they work as super glue that keeps things connected and related together or at least they control and dictate the processes and the forces that keep things related together, like gravity, weak force, strong force, etc.

Third they work as the engine the keeps the universe running.

Fourth they work as a spark that ignites the universe and nature to exist, because without the laws of physics the big bang can't happen, you need a system already in place to initiate the big bang, and that requires some laws of physics to be the in place to start with. They also have other jobs.

5 important conclusions:

First conclusion, our universe can't exist without the laws of physics.

Second conclusion, the laws of physics can't exist without intelligence.

Third conclusion, nature can't exist without the laws of physics, there is nothing to be called nature without the laws of physics.

Fourth conclusion, the laws of physics are a pre-required spark to ignite everything to come to exist, except life.

Fifth conclusion, no complex system can exist without intelligence.

Another BIG question did the laws of physics make themselves? of course they didn't create themselves, so where did they come from? I know you are going to say we don't know.

Was their intelligence to make them in first place, yes, no question about it.

That is only for those who understand the importance, the beauty, the organization, the details, and the value of the laws of physics.

But if you don't understand that, then you need to do so, before judging how the laws of physics came to exist.

Don't fall into the trap and say nature made the laws of physics, because nature can't exist without the laws of physics in first place, nature can't be identified without the pre-exitance of the laws of physics.

You may stop here and go check google, about the equations and formulas of the laws of physics, do you agree on the importance, the beauty, the organization, the details, and the value of the laws of physics? Think about it.

How did the laws of physics get to be there, the way they are, so accurate, so precise, so detailed and so objective, and so beautiful without planning, without understanding, without supervision, without result testing. without directing, without guiding, and without intelligence whatsoever.

If the laws of physics disappear suddenly, then the entire universe instantly will collapse and cease to exist.

Now the BIG dilemma question comes. Which one comes first the chick or the egg?

The answer is: -

If you are a believer, you know God first created the chicken, then the egg came.

If you are atheist, you know Darwin evolution didn't make the egg first.

Now back to the BIG question that has the same dilemma.

Which one comes first, intelligence or the laws of physics?

For atheists the laws of physics were first, without any intelligence whatsoever. Then later intelligence came to exist as result of the right combination, and the right mix of the elements of the periodic table, which happened over long, long, long time by chance after chance after chance… for atheist it is a disaster to say intelligence was first, because that is the instant and final destruction to their entire theology.

For us the believer's intelligence is the AUTHER of the laws of physics.

For us the believer's intelligence is the boss who CREATED the laws of physics.

For us the believer's intelligence is the MOTHER OF ALL MOTHERS.

Ok, they will say maybe there is unlimited number of universes out there, and each one of them has its own laws of physics, will, all that is just escape route to a void saying, yes intelligence is the author of the laws of physics, they are throwing in a theoretical possibility to evade admitting intelligence is the author of the laws of physics, our question now, are the laws of physics a pre- required for any universe to exist? the answer is Yes, and even if there is unlimited number of universes out there they all, no exception, depend on the spark of the laws of physics to bring them up to exist, they all require the laws of physics to provide them their existence.

Even if this possibility is true still it doesn't eliminate the fact that intelligence is the author of the laws of physics.

Now let me show you a double standard they use. They say, they want a physical or scientific evidence that God exists. But when it comes to the unlimited number of universes that may or may not be out there, they only throw it as a theoretical possibility without any type of evidence, they say they only believe in scientific or physical evidence, ok you go get me a scientific or physical evidence that an unlimited number of universes exist out there.

PREPARE FOR THIS BIG ONE, show me by scientific or physical evidence, or empirical evidence that the laws of physics can make themselves, or nature can exist first and then make the laws of physics, we will not accept a theory, assumption, or a theoretical possibility, bring the evidence.

Let me throw this theoretical possibility that in theory it is possible, but practically it is not.

Assuming there are lottery drawings every day in your country, and you are 25 years old, and you play the lottery every day, now theoretically it is possible you will win the lottery every day to the end of your 100 years of life. Practically, you are not going to win the lottery every day in your life, the theoretical existence of a possibility doesn't always make it practically possible, so don't throw in theoretical possibilities and expect us to take it as evidence for your points.

The universe has four dimensions.

We know there are four dimensions in the universe, they are three dimensions for length, width, and height, and the fourth dimension is for time. But those dimensions are worldwide, meaning they always must exist together in the entire world, not in certain areas, they are worldwide.

Now let me surprise you and introduce to you 2 new dimensions, that they only exist in certain limited areas or certain things, your classical way of defining dimensions will not work for these 2.

The 2 new dimensions don't always have to be worldwide, they can exist only in certain things, in certain spaces at a certain time.

First life, life is a new dimension in this world, life is a higher level than the four dimensions of the world.

Second consciousness, consciousness is a new dimension that only exists in certain living things, not all of them.

For atheists you are nothing more than the right combination and the right mixture of the elements of the periodic table that came to exist by chance after chance after chance … over time.

For us believers, you consist of two things, the soul, and the body. But the soul is not part of this universe, it came to this universe for only a limited time then it will depart this universe, and the body exists in a four-dimensional world, three dimensions for space and one for time. But the soul itself is in a higher dimension than these four, the soul is the boss of consciousness, the soul is what makes you, who you are and what you are, not your body, your body is only a biochemical robot, that can't live without your soul, your soul runs and controls the higher functions in your life like, consciousness, love, emotions, saying the truth or lying, anger, morals, etc. the body does the worldly jobs, like carrying stuff, moving stuff, cooking, washing, etc.

For us the believers only your body came to exist from the right combination and the right mixture of the elements of the periodical table. That came to exist by intelligence, by choice, by will and power.

For the atheist's love, morals, emotions, consciousness, etc. is nothing more than the production of the elements of the periodical table.

So, when I do something wrong, don't ask me why? Because it is the wrong combination or the wrong mixture of the elements of the periodical table that made me do the wrong thing, because I only consist of them, blame them, not me. Don't blame my soul.

The elements of the periodical table by themselves can't produce consciousness, love, emotion, moral, etc. You need the soul for that.

If you are going to say it is my fault that I did something wrong, did you get inside my head and see that all the biochemical reactions, were the right ones, all of them?

If so, they have control over everything in my life including consciousness, morals, love. emotions, etc. either way you still must blame them not me, because they gave me the power of free will, the power to lie. And the power to do bad stuff. But they didn't make sure I don't abuse the power of free will.

By the way

Why did the elements of the periodic table give me the free will?

Why did the elements of the periodic table give me the power to love?

Why did the elements of the periodic table give me the power to lie?

Why did the elements of the periodic table give me the power to feel emotions?

Why did the elements of the periodic table give me the power to enjoy things?

Why did the elements of the periodic table give me the power to understand things?

Why did the elements of the periodic table give me the power to do many things?

If they did give me all those powers, they would have made it impossible for everyone to lie or do something Wrong, but they didn't, when they could've.

Hey you the elements of the periodic table I'm so mad at you, because you gave us the humans the power to lie and the power to do bad stuff, when you had the keys in your hands to shut off those power, but you didn't, in reality you are the bad guys , and we the humans, are only victims of your actions, you handed us on a golden plate the powers to do wrong, what the hick was wrong with you guys?

My answer, they didn't, and they can't. Your soul did, and that is the purpose of human life.

Time

The second most important component of the universe is time. Without time nothing can come to exist. Without time the universe will not have a chance after the Big Bang to expand, grow and become universe without time nothing will exist. Maybe the laws of physics will be there, but on their own somewhere else, just a reminder the laws of physics have absolute authority, and control over time.

By the way some people think time is just a concept in our minds, no time is a real existing thing in the universe, and we made the units to measure time, second, minute, hour, etc.

Also, we made the units to measure distance, mass, and other stuff.

I want to throw in a surprise question about time that may have never been asked before.

But first let us agree that our universe is finite (limited), then everything in it is also finite or limited, no exception. Do you agree?

If you agree everything in the universe is limited, then time is finite or limited, and it is getting consumed by the second, and eventually we will run out of time, meaning that all the time in the universe will get consumed, because it is limited, it can't last forever, anything limited can't last forever.

I know you want to scream in my face and say time will keep running forever, it doesn't end,

Your scream is only an assumption, time is limited, and it may run out suddenly without warning.

The big question now, what will happen if time runs out tomorrow?

Try to find out on your own. This is a big and deep question.

Another way of asking the same question about time running out, is to ask, does everything in the universe have expiration date, no exception?

If yes, how do you know time will not expire tomorrow, or how do you know the laws of physics will not expire tomorrow?

Space

The third most fundamental component of the universe is space. If space did not exist, then nothing would exist. You won't exist and me won't exist. If space did not exist, where are you going to put all the galaxies, where you are going to put the sun, where you are going to put planet earth, and you and me, so without a space, absolutely no stuff or matter can exist, except maybe for the laws of physics, which are in their own existence.

The stuff or matter

The fourth most fundamental component of the universe is the staff and everything else, but here we are only going to talk about matter, if matter did not exist then galaxies would not exist, the sun would not exist, and Planet earth would not exist. You and I would not exist so maybe there will be an empty universe, OK there is the law of physics, there is time, and there is space, but no matter to do anything. What are you going to do? What can you get when there is no matter, to do things, like the planets, and everything else?

OK, so those four fundamental components. I call them the four brothers or the four twins because they are literally twins and must be together to make life, if one of them was missing, me and you will also be missing.

Here comes the BIG question. The question that's going to make it or break it.

How did these four twin brothers get packaged together and pushed out through the Big Bang exactly at the same time, exactly in the same fraction of a second. And they were told hey guys, you are brothers be nice to each other work in harmony and peace with each other. Don't you guys fight and go make all the stuff that you can make, and the laws of physics will be the boss who controls everything and who has authority and power over everything, and they're going to be the police officers who is going to control everything and who is going to tell every particle and every sub particle how to behave what they can do, and what they cannot do, for example they will tell the electron you are an electron you must behave this way you must have this charge you must have this size you must have this mass and you must be running all the time in circles nonstop and don't you dare to take a break, no break for you guys. You must keep working forever with no breaks for you guys, if you guys take a break you are going to break everything, yes everything, so you guys keep running in circles forever, because your running will keep everything up and running. If you guys sit down for 1 MS everything is going to collapse.

The protons and the neutrons were told by the laws of physics hey guys, you go inside the nuclei and sit there, and don't you dare to come out, well you can come out if there is a huge impact hits the atom, really, huge one.

But the laws of physics have only limited control not absolute control over living things like humans, because we choose to buy a house or rent. We choose to buy a red shirt or a blue shirt. We choose to buy a car or not, etc. The laws of physics do not control those choices, we do, the laws of physics do not decide if I'm going to be a human or something else. that was decided by other decision prosses.

Back to the big question of how and why did those four twins get packaged together and pushed out through the big bang to make everything that they can make, so what do you think? How did they get packaged together and pushed out through the big bang and why?

Just for fun, they got delivered through the big bang, not through USPS, UPS, FEDEX, etc. Because they didn't exist back then, ok just kidding.

There were three possibilities out there: -

first one: there were only those four components out there, and somehow, they got pushed out through the Big Bang to make everything.

The second: is that more components were there, and only these four were randomly pushed out through the big bang, or intentionally only them were chosen.

The third: there was unlimited number of components out there, and only those four were selected, ok how did this happen, and why? you're going to say by chance by, coincidence, by luck, by whatever you say, do you have evidence? to say by chance, by coincidence, by luck, etc.

My answer

Those four components were pre-made by intelligence, will, and power for their mission.

99.99%

50% OF 50%

Yes, this is the name of the chapter, I know it is strange to name a chapter with numbers. But I want you to remember these two numbers forever, I will tell you their importance shortly.

First let me tell you that I do believe in an evolution that was planned and supervised.

Let's look back, you were little kids, and you were taught Darwin evolutionary theory, the way they did. But they held a very big, very important parts, they didn't tell you, that by coincidence 99.99% of the random mutations were the right one, for the right reason, at the right time, and they didn't tell you only less than 1% were the wrong one, for the wrong reason, at the wrong time.

If they did, you would not swallow it, even when you were a kid. They gave you Darwin evolutionary theory as a whole package, and you didn't have the chance to open the package, and check the components for yourself, you didn't have the chance to see that, it was consisting of 99.99% the right ones by coincidence, and only less than 1% the wrong owns by coincidence. If you did, even when you were a kid, you would not swallow it, you will through it in the trash can where it belongs.

Did you know that according to Darwin evolutionary theory, by coincident, yes by coincident, ok may be by luck, or by chance 99.99% of the random mutations, were the right one for the right reason at the right time, by coincident, I must say it a gain by coincident, did you get it, by coincident.

Darwin evolutionary theory is a scam, Darwin evolutionary theory is identity theft.

Although this 99.99% number is not stated officially in plain words, in Darwin evolutionary theory, it is there by implication, and I will explain that later in this chapter.

Now I know you want to scream in my face and challenge this 99.99% number, before you do so, this is my big challenge for you, are you ready for it?

Darwin evolutionary theory works only by random mutations, or undirected unguided mutations, ok you are going to say what about natural selection, I call it obvious selection, natural selection (obvious selection), is nothing more than an obvious point, natural selection says, survival is for the fittest, actually that is wrong, survival is for the fit not the fittest, they lied to you when they said survival is for the fittest, the truth is survival is for the fit.

It is an obvious point, that if you don't fit in for life, you will not survive. They took this obvious point and made it a part of a theory, you can't take an obvious point and make it part of a theory, obvious stuff is obvious stuff, it can't be used for theories or science. So don't use your natural selection in any theory. We don't need obvious stuff as a part of theories.

This is my challenge to you:

Show me in the older fossil records were only 50% of the species have only 50% of their organs, the wrong organ, in the wrong place, of the wrong size, of the wrong tissue, for the wrong reason.

I'm willing to gamble everything for this challenge, I will put all my eggs in one basket for you to break, I will abandon my faith in God, and instantly I will become the most hard-core atheist, I will bet all my money, I will be everything you want me to be. You show me in the fossil record were only 50% of the species had only 50% of their organs, the wrong organ in the wrong place for the wrong reason, of the wrong size, of the wrong tissue. Ok, this one was a big one let me give you a smaller challenge, can you explain how life came to be without using these 2 words (random and luck). Did you know the 2 words random, and luck are 2 of atheist's gods?

YOU WILL FAIL TO SHOW ME THAT 50% OF 50% NUMBER, Do I NEED TO SHOW YOU THE 99.99% NUMBER? NO, I DON'T.

You can't show me that. But I can show you in any fossil record that 99.99% of their organs, the right organ for the right reason in the right place of the right size and of the right tissue.

How did this happen?

Yes, I forgot by coincident, by chance, by luck, by probability...etc.

Now let's have a look at Darwin evolutionary theory, first we need to do exercise. Please get yourself two big photo frames, one has the photo of a single cell living thing in it, put it to your left, and the second much bigger one that has the photo of a full human body with all the internal organs shown on it, put it to your right.

Remember the single cell photo, is the photo your grandpa who lived long, long, long time ago,

Say hi grandpa. The full human photo is you, that's just according to the atheists.

Let us see what it took to get from your grandpa, on your left to you, it took lots and lots and lots and lots of exceptional luck.

There was your grandpa and billions of random or unguided, undirected mutations, nothing was systematic about it.

Then random mutations started happening, but luck was right there for them 99.99% of the time. That was only for your grandpas, you can't have that much luck, if you get to have that much luck you will be the only one who keeps winning the lottery, and everybody else will be mad at you, or asking you if they could borrow your luck for only one day, and that is why Darwin evolutionary theory took the luck away from you. I know you have been asking all the time where is my luck? Now you know.

Let us first, have a list of some of the organs of the human body: -

1.   Adrenal glands.

2.   Anus

3.   Appendix

4.   Bladder (urinary)

5.   Bones

6.   Bone marrow (spongy part of the bone)

7.   Brain

8.   Bronchi (tubes in the lungs)

9.   Diaphragm (muscle of breathing)

10.   Ears

11.   Esophagus (food pipe)

12.   Eyes

13.   Fallopian tubes

14.   Gallbladder

15.   Genitals

16.   Heart

17.   Hypothalamus (in the brain)

18.   Joints

19.   Kidneys

20.   Large intestine

21.   Larynx (voice box)

22.   Liver

23.   Lungs

24.   Lymph nodes

25.   Mammary glands

26.   Mesentery (covering of the intestines)

27.   Mouth

28.   Nasal cavity

29.   Nose

30.   Ovaries

31.   Pancreas

32.   Pineal gland

33.   Parathyroid glands

34.   Pharynx

35.   Pituitary gland

36.   Prostate

37.   Rectum

38.   Salivary glands

39.   Skeletal muscles

40.   Skin

41.   Small intestine

42.   Spinal cord

43.   Spleen

44.   Stomach

45.   Teeth

46.   Thymus gland

47.   Thyroid

48.   Trachea

49.	Tongue

50.	Ureters

51.	Urethra

52.	Uterus

53.	Human skeleton

54.	Ligaments (connect muscles to bones)

55.	Tendons (connect bones to bones)

56.	Blood cells

57.	Vagina

58.	Hair

59.	The vestibular system of the ear

60.	Placenta

61.	Testes

62.	Nails

63.	Vas deferens

64.	Seminal vesicles

65.	Bulbourethral glands

66.	Penis

67.	Scrotum

68.	Parathyroid glands

69.	Thoracic ducts

70.	Arteries

71.	Veins

72.	Capillaries

73.	Lymphatic vessels

74.	Tonsils (Waldeyer's ring of tissues)

75.	Nerves

76.	Subcutaneous tissue

77.	Olfactory epithelium (nose)

78.	Cerebellum

Watch for the coming scam.

You got all these organs in your body because of random mutations and lots, and lots, and lots of luck, there was no systematic way for you to get them, because the word systematic requires a system initiator or organizer. And we know systems can't initiate or make themselves.

 Now they are going to trick you saying that: (by time our bodies started to learn how to keep the right mutations and get rid of the wrong ones). This is the core of their scam.

Any learning process requires understanding, comparing, judging, and acting on the judgment. But back then those functions were not available to Darwin evolutionary theory, they required intelligence. Darwin evolutionary theory had only one single tool random mutation, but it had also, lots, lots, lots, and lots of luck, I promise you will never have that much luck, I promise you will never win the lottery every day in your life, when your grandpas died, they took all that luck with them to the grave.

A shout out for the fiction righters, can someone of you write story about how lucky our grandpas were to get all those organs by luck, and now we are praying for some luck, and it is hard to find, ok folks, maybe they buried all that luck somewhere in a treasure box in the desert and we need to go find it.

<h1 style="text-align:center">Back to reality</h1>

Ok folks, atheists now are blaming us for not understanding the power of luck, luck, luck, yes, I forgot luck is one of their gods, we must understand the most important two words in their vocabulary, they are RANDOM and LUCK.

You believers out there don't underestimate the powers of random and luck, you came to be a human by these two powers, if you, through away these two powers in the trash can, atheists will get mad and sue you. And you don't want to get sued? Do you?

Atheists make the false claim that they only believe in scientific evidence. But their biggest blind belief is in the powers of random and luck, and for them no greater belief exists out there than the belief of the powers of (random and luck), period.

Every single one of this organs is a very complex system, connected to the other organs through another very complex system, and the higher functions in your body are connected by another complex system to your brain which is the most complex of all, you got all that by the powers of random and luck, so whenever you needed an organ, the powers of random and luck gave it to you, right away in a golden plate, actually I'm assuming it was a golden plate, it may be I'm making stuff up by saying golden plate, so please when you read this book, don't tell everybody, I made stuff up, (the golden plate thing).

Ok when you needed every organ to be in the right place, the powers of random and luck came up and granted you that for free, and they didn't leave you. they stood by you all the way to the end, just in case you were going to need them, even when you were sleeping, they were standing there by you, they didn't sleep, you didn't have to call them or pray for them, they gave you everything even before you ask for it.

And when you needed the right size for any organ, they were right there, before you asked.

And when you needed the right shape of the organ, they were right there, before you asked.

And when you needed the right tissue for the organ, they were right there, before you asked.

And when you needed the right function of the organ, they were right there, before you asked.

And when you needed the right connections of the organ, they were right there, before you asked.

And when you needed the right complexity of the organ, they were right there, before you asked.

How do I know this? Maybe I started to believe in the powers of random and luck. BIG LAUGH.

I'm going to take the example of the eye.

When you were a multi cell organism, you didn't know that there was light out there, and you can develop an eye to benefit from it and use it for your advantage. You didn't know what light is, what is its properties, is it harmful, or beneficial, what do you need to start using it for your benefit. But random mutations and luck took care of all that for you, for free. Don't worry you will not receive a bill from random mutations, I do guarantee that for you. Relax dude. You were in your pajamas watching your favorite cartoon, and the magic of mutations and luck was working for you for free. You didn't have to do anything or worry about anything. The powers of random and luck were there for you, for free.

Can you imagine we are trying to make a sensor like your eye, to detect something that we know nothing about, and even we don't know if it is out there or not. Totally by random processes, then after many random trials we get the right sensor for the right job, that we didn't know anything about it.

I'm going to assume that you are engineer, you step in your boss's office you tell him give me lots of random tools, I want to design a sensor to detect an unknown thing out there, and tell him also, we don't know if it is out there or not in first place. And tell him, yes, we will benefit from it. Can you, do it? Darwin evolution did it for your eye, your ear, and all your senses, etc.

How did Darwin evolutionary theory produce a sensor (your eye) to detect light and benefit you from it, when it didn't know anything about light?

Atheists will say you believers, you call yourselves believers, but you still don't believe in the powers of random and luck. You just need to add these to powers to your belief, and everything will be fine. My response will be you need to add to your belief the power of intelligence, instead of that.

What was the percentage of the wrong random mutation?

When we check the fossil record, or the body of any creature we see that less than 1% of the random mutations were the wrong ones, and 99.99% were always the right ones. Don't try to say they developed a system to get rid of the wrong ones and keep the right ones, because that requires to have the system planted in place before the first random mutation takes place, to start checking, comparing, deciding and acting, from the very start, you can't have this system at a later point, and then when you become a full human, all the evidence for the existence of that system is erased from inside our cells, that system exists in your imagination only, and the leave us to wonder exactly how complex was that system, how big its parts were, what was its forms and mechanisms of getting information, comparing, deciding, acting and guaranteeing that only the right ones will remain and the wrong ones will be executed or hanged on a pole downtown. Just kidding.

Darwin evolutionary theory betrayed all of us: -

It didn't give us eyes in the in the back and the side of our heads to see everything around us, and it will not.

It didn't give us wings to fly instead of buying cars and polluting the environment, and it will not, it gave them to the birds, and said to us. Ok humans, you are not going to have wings.

It didn't give us a super strong immune system, and it will not.

It didn't give our skin the ability to absorb sunlight and convert it to energy, to use. And it will not.

It didn't give us the power to run fast like the cheetah or even faster to avoid using cars, and it will not.

It gave us the power to lie and do bad stuff, it should have kept these two powers away from us, but it didn't. I'm so, so, so, mad at Darwin evolutionary theory, because it gave us the power to lie and do bad stuff. It should have kept them away from us, what the hick was wrong with you Darwin evolutionary theory? Were you stupid? Or did you intend that for us?

Assuming Darwin evolutionary theory is going to give us wings, what will it take?

It will take lots, lots, lots of random mutations working together in collaboration at the same time, not everyone on its own. But that is impossible because the word collaboration is against random.

You need random mutations to start preparing your brain to handle wings and flying.

You need random mutations to start adjusting your body shape for flying.

You need random mutations to start growing the right wings, of the right strength, in the right place of your body.

You need random mutations to start connecting your wings with the blood supply.

You need random mutations to start connecting your wings to the nerves. And many more.

All these random mutations MUST happen individually each on its own, but by luck and only by luck, they must be synchronized and working in collaboration with each other only by luck, only by luck, only by luck. DID YOU GET IT? ONLY BY LUCK.

Ok stop. What if we only wanted eyes in the back of our heads, what do you think is needed? I think the same thing with the wings.

And yes, folks I don't trust random mutations and luck to give me even a single hair, let alone this great, beautiful, complex, smart, loving body, etc. Do you?

Let me assume the average human life is about 90 years, what would be the case if evolution gave us 10 times that average to live (900 years), yes that will be a disaster, what if it gave us only 9 years to live, (10 times less). Yes that will be a disaster, yes folks I should start believing in the powers of random and luck. The same age scenario applies for all species. A gain the powers of random and luck.

What if the average human size was 10 times greater, that would be disaster, what if it was 10 times smaller, that would be disaster. A gain the powers random and luck gave us the right size.

If we evolved from apes

Why didn't we keep the ability to live outside in the rain 24 hours a day, just like our grandpas did?

Why didn't we keep tough skin to protect us from mosquito bites, just like our grandpas did?

Our grandpas (the apes) their adulthood is about one year. But ours is about 18 years old, if we became adults in one year like our grandpas (the apes), that would be a disaster. Imagine at 10 years old, you already have grand kids. How did all these changes happen? By the powers of random and luck.

Ok folks, could someone tell me, were we created by the power of God or the powers of random and luck?

Ok folks, I need Darwin evolutionary theory phone number, to call her and ask her to take away these 2 powers from us. The power to lie and the power to do bad stuff. And I Will pay her a penny for that, I have the penny right now in my hand. It gave us these 2 powers in the first place, do you agree? If yes, then blame it on her, or ask her to come take them away.

Why don't we find this?

You will never see a creature that evolution gave him his eyes below his mouth, yes folks this was by the powers of random and luck, you will never see a creature his mouth in the back of his head, yes folks this was by the powers of random and luck, you will never see a creature his legs on his back not under his belly. Yes, folks this was by the powers of random and luck. You will never see a creature trying to grow extra eyes on his sides or legs. Yes, folks this was by the powers of random and luck. I can keep going to mention every organ. But I don't need to do so. You folks now understand the powers of random and luck.

Ok, you stop are going to tell us something about the complex systems in our bodies, and how the powers of random and luck got them there? May be in the second edition of the book, if I needed to.

Theoretically in the fossil record, we suppose to find that the earliest ones had 99.99% of their organs, the wrong organ in the wrong place, of the wrong size, of the wrong tissue, for the wrong reason. But you will not, then after a while this percentage will drop to 90%, then it will drop to 80%. Then it will drop to 70%, then to 60%, then to 50%. And so, on until it gets to 10% then to less than 1%.

But all you see in the fossil record or in real life, is that 99.99% of them are the right ones, for the right reason, in the right place, of the right size, of the right tissue.

You will never see that Darwin evolution tried to get the dinosaurs back on track. And it never will.

You think we evolved from apes, I'm going to assume that 1000 000 years ago we started evolving from apes to humans, why didn't another group start to evolve 900 000 years ago, then why didn't another group start to evolve 800 000 years ago, and so on to 100 000 years ago, to 10 000 years ago. Humans and every specie got only one chance to evolve, and never a second chance, by now we supposed to be walking on the streets saying, look this group will take them another 50 000 years to become full humans, and this group will take them another 100 000 years to become full humans, and so on. Also, that will apply to all species. But you are not going to see any of that, all species had one chance only.

You are not going to see an animal who managed to get 90% smart brains like humans, another one 80% like humans, then another one 70% like humans, and so on, you will not see that.

You are not going to see an animal who managed to get 90% developed language like humans, another one 80% like humans, then another one 70% like humans, and so on, you will not see that.

In fact, all the creatures you see in the world have huge gap in their intelligence and language capabilities compared to humans when most of them existed millions of years before humans, but Darwin evolutionary theory didn't grant them that, it did that for the humans only. Why?

The BIG question now, was that by power of intelligence? Or by the powers of random and luck?

If you are atheist, the most hated word for you in this book is intelligence. No rational person will hate the word intelligence, intelligence is the boss of love.

In fact, for us believers, to believe anything it must be coherent with intelligence, rationality, logic, and common sense.

They lied to you.

Let me take the example from when we started evolving from apes to humans, it only takes a very short window of time for the proper mutation to occur, and that is exactly when the sperm hits the egg, before they start multiplying cells. If it happens before, it will be limited to the egg, or limited to the sperm, it can't happen separately for both, if it did happen separately, it is of course bad, it is good only at the time when the sperm hits the egg before the start of multiplying the cells. The right one must happen when the sperm meets the egg before the multiplying of the cells.

All the random mutations that happen in your body later will be limited to certain cells in your body, and that is bad for you and your offsprings.

The only time to get the right random mutations is at the moments when the sperm meets the egg before they start multiplying, and that is a very small window.

If you add all these small windows of time. From your grandpa the ape to you I promise it will not add up to one year, so where is the millions of years. Because all mutations outside this small window, they all are the wrong ones, and they don't cont.

Now I'm going to assume you are the first one who started evolving from an ape to a human. The problem now is how to keep all your offsprings synchronized with the same level of advancement, across all individuals and generations without exception. To make sure all individuals get to become full humans, all at the same time, when the single tool available is individual random mutations, not wholesale, or synchronized mutations.

Ok you are generation one, you get to have 3 kids they are generation 2, then each one of them get to have 3 kids they are generation 3, then you keep going down to the final humans, for example happened to be generation 100 000.

All these generations kept their advancement synchronized by luck, there was no planning, no directing, no guiding. You will not see any group become fully humans, then another group, then another group, at different times. How did this happen? By the powers of random and luck.

Maximum Insanity

No greater insanity can be out there than this insanity, that we got to feel emotions, have intelligence, have consciousness, and have love by the work of Mr. Dirt, Mr. Random, and Mr. Luck.

Please imagine yourself, you are the only one on planet earth with no other forms of life around you, you are walking on dirt, you hold in your hand some dirt, and you start asking, what is this how did I get here. Now you have no idea that you were made from this dirt by the help of only 2 employees, Mr. Random and Mr. Luck, how did that happen?

Once upon a time, there was your grandpa Mr. Dirt, living alone on planet earth, and he felt lonely, for millions of years he was alone, but he remembered that he has to other brothers, that he could call on them, to give him a company and do something, and he remembered their names, Mr. Random and Mr. Luck.

And he started calling on them, and calling, and calling, and finally they heard their brother (Mr. Dirt) was calling ,and they came running from far, far ,far planet, and it took them millions of years to get to their brother, and hug him, and apologized for being away for so long, and they promised they will stay together because they are brothers, they should stay together and help each other for free, and to make everything they want together for free, and never charge their brothers. But we humans do.

Then Mr. Dirt said to his brothers, Guys let's do something instead of just keep chatting forever, we got all the time we need. They replied. Do something what are you talking about dude? he said, I got the material and I got you my brothers, I will supply you with all the material you want for free, and you guys, your names tell me, you can come up with something from all this material I have here, by the way brothers your names are so beautiful and they have a lot of energy in them. I love your names, brothers if we keep working together, We can make something like life, when they heard the word life they were shocked, they said explain to us what is life, and he started to explaining what life is, and it took him long time to explain, what life is and what it can do, they said brother, we would help you do anything else but not life there is going to be suffering there, stop it please brother, and he kept telling them about everything good in life. But they weren't listening at all. But Mr. Dirt has kept his best secret for last, (LOVE), As soon as his brothers heard the word "love", they jumped up from their seats and started singing and dancing, and right away, they said to him. Yes, Brother we will work with you, you came up with the greatest thing in the world, well will work with you no matter how hard it is, and no matter how long it is going to take.

Just a hint for fiction writers, I know some of you will like such a story, and want to write something like it, but this one has copy writes.

You may write to: The info on the copy right page.

Now let's stop fiction and go back to reality.

That Dirt you are holding in your hand is your grandpa Mr. dirt, he was working with his other 2 brothers Mr. random and Mr. luck for billions of years, seven days a week, 24 hours a day, they didn't take a single day off, they didn't take any holiday off, they were the hardest workers on planet earth, They didn't take Christmas off, they didn't take 4th of July off, they just kept working to get you there, and once they did, they said that's enough, we are not going to make any more life. We are going to retire, and they did retire, and lived ever happily in their retirement.

Your ingredients

You have unofficial ingredients label placed on your forehead says, you were made from planet earth ingredients, by the hands of Mr. random and Mr. luck, they own the factory that made you, and gave you all your powers including feeling love and emotions, they gave you intelligence. But they didn't give you wings. And they will not.

They gave you everything you need to live your life, they gave you:

Eyes to see without planning, without guiding, and without directing.

ears to hear without planning, without guiding, and without directing.

Legs to walk without planning, without guiding, and without directing.

Hands to use without planning, without guiding, and without directing.

nose to smell without planning, without guiding, and without directing.

Mouth to use without planning, without guiding, and without directing.

Tung to talk without planning, without guiding, and without directing.

Stomach to use without planning, without guiding, and without directing.

Kidney to use without planning, without guiding, and without directing.

Skin to use without planning, without guiding, and without directing.

Heart to use without planning, without guiding, and without directing.

Lungs to use without planning, without guiding, and without directing.

Liver to use without planning, without guiding, and without directing.

Intestine to use without planning, without guiding, and without directing.

Fingers to use without planning, without guiding, and without directing.

Nails to use without planning, without guiding, and without directing.

Joints to use without planning, without guiding, and without directing.

Nerves to use without planning, without guiding, and without directing.

Brains to use without planning, without guiding, and without directing.

All the cells in your body without planning, without guiding, and without directing.

All the organs in your body are without planning, without guiding, and without directing. You just got everything from these three brothers (Mr. Dirt, Mr. Random, and Mr. Luck).

You got love without planning, without guiding, and without directing.

You got intelligence without planning, without guiding, and without directing.

You got the emotions without planning, without guiding, and without directing.

According to atheists you are a piece of dirt, you are nothing more than dirt.

I'm going to give the atheists the last name (Mr. and Mrs. DIRT). because their grandpa is Mr. Dirt, please atheists don't feel offended, that is exactly who you are.

We the believers, we are the people of the spirit, not you guys, because you don't believe in the spirit, you must stop using the word spirit, because for you it is only a lie, in your mind, so stop lying or repeating the lie, leave the word spirit for us, we believe we have a spirit, and that is what makes us humans(the spirit), not dirt.

Please step outside and grab some dirt and put it somewhere in your living room and keep looking at it every day and ask yourself every day.

Can this dirt produce intelligence? Can this dirt produce consciousness?

Can this dirt produce emotions? Can this dirt produce love?

For atheists Yes it can with the help of time, random, and luck.

Some atheist's arguments

Why don't we see God?

You only can see what's part of this universe, but God is not part of this universe, and that's also why you can't see the soul, because it is not part of this universe.

They ask why did intelligent designer put an entertainment system with a sewage system?

The answer is what kind of random powers can combine 2 functions in one organ, it is better to combine 2 private functions in one organ if possible. How did the power of random figure that out?

They ask why there is evil in the world?

the answer for this question is divided to three parts:

Part one

Because all this life is a test, how you are going to act in good times, and in bad times, when you are sick, and when you are healthy, when you are happy, and when you are sad, when you are rich and when you are poor, etc. That is why God gave you the free will, (you didn't get the free will from the elements of the periodic table). And that is why this life is short roughly about 90 years, God could've given us to live 1000 years or 10000 years, but that will be too long test,

Part two

If there was no evil in this world, would you still choose not to believe in God? If yes, why are you asking, why evil exists? Don't let evil stop you from believing in God, don't let evil be your boss, (my boss is intelligence), telling you what to believe, and what not to believe, don't fall in the trap of evil, don't let evil force on you, that your grandpa was an ape, and all forms of life came to exist by the powers of random and luck. Random and luck will not give you wings to fly.

Part three

In the second life God will guarantee for every on in heaven the following:

Endless life, you will live forever, death doesn't exist in heaven.

You will have constant uninterrupted happiness, constant uninterrupted joy, constant uninterrupted pleasure, everything you wish for instantly granted,

And the list is too long for me to mention, and of course in heaven there is no evil, not even for one single second.

Some atheists say they don't believe in superstition, or the supernatural, why do you?

First, we need them to explain to us what they mean by superstition and supernatural, do they mean anything outside this universe is superstition and supernatural, or what do they exactly mean. You are living inside this universe, (inside this box), you must think outside the box, to understand there may be something else out there, don't limit existence to our universe only, if you do that is a terrible mistake. If you do, then you shouldn't believe anything existed before the big bang. But if nothing existed before the big bang, then where did it come from and why?

Some atheists ask why religion is abused?

Nothing in life is abuse free, absolutely nothing. And the most abused 3 venues in life are politics, religion, and finance, and it will remain this way forever, science is abused by certain people, to tell you that intelligence is not required to make the laws of physics, but it is required to discover them, understand them, and use them.

Atheists say why so many religions, which one is true?

It is obvious people will differ in their thinking, and understanding about God, because, he is not here inside this universe, and most people don't have the power, the time, the energy, and resources, to check their concept about God, is the right one or not, the answer in short words, it is a human error. In my next book I will tell which religion I follow, and what are my arguments for my religion, very fresh arguments never been used before, why I choose this religion, and how you may choose yours.

Some atheists say there is no evidence that God exists?

The evidence for God's existence is only logical or circumstantial evidence not physical evidence.

The type of evidence you are thinking of (physical evidence) is what's used for testable stuff, but God is untestable, the evidence you are looking for, is physical evidence that can detect God, but God is outside this universe, he can't be detected. Our evidence for God is only logical or circumstantial evidence not physical evidence, meaning if you look at the laws of physics, you know there must be intelligence to make them, if you look at the complex life forms, you know they were made by intelligence.

This book is a gift for humanity. If you benefited from this book, please share it with everyone you know, let them have the same benefit you did, share it on your social media, share it with your colleagues. Let's get this noble book for every human soul. Let's get the message out there.

If you think this is a bad book. You must warn everybody not to buy this book, warn them on your social media, not to waste their money and time on this book, get your message out there.

Please wait for my next book in which I will reveal my religion, why and how did I choose it from among so many religions.

By the way I'm over 50 years old, I have been living in the lovely town, Austin, TX, for more than 2 decades. My initials are N.A., You may see me one day in a coffee shop, I always wear simple casual clothes, nothing fancy.

I will wait a few years to see how atheists will try to refute my book, then I will refute their refuting trials. I still have surprising points for them.

Avery strange point

Ladies you have been lied to and scammed, you have been told, that you women are half the society, that is a scam. Women are more than half the society, women are majority, men are minority, so guys be nice to women, we are outnumbered, if women start a political party, they will win every election. Why are women majority? Because 2 million men are in jail, and only 100k women in jail, every day in America about 40 men get killed, and only 3 women, every day in America more than 100 people commit suicide, about 80% are men, every day in America more than 250 people die of drug overdose, about 66% are men.

How is this strange point related to religion? The solution will be in my next book.

I wish everybody great blessings. Goodbye, See you in my next book, thanks.